ENDC

"**Groundbreaking** insights to heal your heart! A **profound** guide to the freedom of deep forgiveness."

> Bill Johnson
> Senior Pastor of Bethel Church in Redding, CA

"This is by far the **most effective** forgiveness book I have ever read. I give away many copies every week to help those struggling to forgive!"

> Barbara Solis
> Pastor of Family Counseling at Peoples Church in Fresno, CA, the largest megachurch in Central California

"As someone who has taught about forgiveness many times, Dr. Allen gave me tools I've never considered to the point that I took several moments to freshly forgive several people. If you feel stuck in moving on from ways you've been hurt, or if you teach others how to forgive, I'm confident you'll find fresh ways forward here."

> Dave Schmelzer
> Executive Director of Blue Ocean Faith
> Founding Pastor of Reservoir Church in Cambridge, MA
> Author of *Not the Religious Type: Confessions of a Turncoat Atheist*

"As a practicing family medicine physician, I see firsthand the effects of unforgiveness on personal health and on social relationships. As an avid reader of Christian books, I also see the superficial manner in which the resolution of unforgiveness is treated, as if a simple prayer or declaration can remove the emotional burdens of unforgiveness in a moment. Dr. Allen's book, *The Language of Deep Forgiveness*, uniquely supplies a thorough understanding of the subject of forgiveness, and workable steps for breaking free from the habits of unforgiveness, using psychological, theological and scientific approaches. I heartily encourage the reader to study and apply the principles contained in this excellent work, as I have done for myself and for my patients."

John Erickson, MD

"Oh no, not another book on forgiveness! I've read all the bestsellers on the subject and still haven't been able to apply any of them. I tried so many times to really forgive, saying forgiveness prayers as emphatically as possible. But ultimately, I knew in my heart something was missing. I resigned myself to having repression as my lifelong friend. Then I was surprised by this wonderful book that gave me new hope and the fresh tools I needed to make several dramatic forgiveness breakthroughs that have forever changed my life. I'm so grateful for the help it provided me!"

Kathy O., L.C.S.W.

"Forgiveness, a multifaceted task that affects the very foundations of our wellness as people. The ability to forgive is not just a simple and easy exercise in saying the words, 'I forgive.' In his book, Dr. Allen shows us the words we use are integral to our core ability to accomplish forgiveness and be free from the chains of unforgiveness. I highly recommend that you enter into this exploration of forgiveness and learn how to address the most important aspects to yourself and finally be free of the affliction of long term offense and unforgiveness. I used his book as a study to lead myself and others into the freedom of absolute forgiveness."

Mark Van Dyke
Executive Pastor of University Vineyard Church

"Immensely clear and insightful! Anyone struggling with issues surrounding forgiveness would do well to start with Dr. Allen's book."

John Carter, PhD
Retired Professor of Clinical Psychology

The Language of Deep Forgiveness

Break Free from Struggling to Accept the Unacceptable

By Dr. Allen Gee

ForgiveWell.com

Purple Dove Press

To my precious wife, Erica Christine.

CONTENTS

Endorsements i

Contents ix

Preface x

Introduction 1

    Overview 2

    Jennifer's Story 3

1. The Significance of Language 7

    Practicing Deep Forgiveness 14

2. Two Natural Laws 19

3. The Acceptance Conundrum 27

4. Your Personal Brain 43

5. What Forgiveness Is Not 51

6. The Two Pillars 55

Conclusion 59

Appendix 65

    Dictionary Definitions of Forgiveness 66

    Study Guide 68

References 71

About the Author 73

PREFACE

I have created an innovative method to help people forgive more deeply and quickly so that they may live with inner peace, happiness, and spiritual vitality. It has enabled many to experience breakthrough and freedom after years, even decades, of struggling with bitterness and resentment. My approach is a unique blend of insights from the fields of Christian spirituality, theology, clinical psychology, psycho-linguistics, and brain science.

This book was developed out of several diverse areas of my life: my doctoral education and training in clinical psychology, my work as a spiritual life coach and seminar speaker, my scientific research and engineering in the field of artificial intelligence, and my own personal experiences in wrestling through the issue of forgiveness.

Although written from a Christian perspective, the forgiveness techniques described within can benefit everyone regardless of their religious beliefs. Many have found this material life-changing! My hope is that it will be of immense value to everyone who wishes to walk in the freedom of deep forgiveness.

ACKNOWLEDGEMENTS

I am grateful for the help in reading and editing this manuscript given by Christine Gee, Dave Schmelzer, John Erickson, Mark and Barbara Van Dyke, Christiana Oswald, Wanell Sause, Eric Aslakson, and John Carter.

INTRODUCTION

Everything should be made as simple as possible, but not simpler.

— Albert Einstein

Language etches the grooves through which your thoughts must flow.

— Noam Chomsky

May these words of my mouth and this meditation of my heart
>   be pleasing in your sight,
>   LORD, my Rock and my Redeemer.

— Psalms 19:14

Overview

In this book, you will find the answers to these important questions:

1. Why is forgiveness so difficult?

2. What are the two pillars of forgiveness?

3. How does the precise language you use to think about forgiveness in your mind affect how deeply you actually forgive in your heart?

4. Why are declarations of forgiveness toward others, including those spoken in prayer, often insufficient in producing lasting freedom from unforgiveness?

5. How can you speak forgiveness more effectively?

6. What can you do when forgiveness seems to require you to accept those offenders you consider unacceptable?

Jennifer's Story

Jennifer's mind was caught up in a whirlpool of rage, threatening to drown her soul. *How can I possibly forgive him? What he did to me was so terrible and inexcusable! All I honestly want is for him to suffer and die!* Her anger had become all-consuming, overwhelming, uncontainable. It was more than she had felt in a long time, perhaps more than she had ever felt. And yet another part of her was utterly shocked by its ferocity, stunned by the realization of just how much intense hatred she was capable of feeling toward another human being.

But this man had severely betrayed her trust. What made matters worse was that he was also an authority figure in a position to profoundly affect her life. He had abused his power and treated her unjustly. And it seemed there was little she could do about it. Feeling helplessness in the grip of such unexpected injustice only enraged her further. Because she had once considered him a friend and mentor, so intense was the pain of his betrayal.

Jennifer tried to resolve the situation through open dialog. She approached him with graciousness, hoping that reason might prevail between them. But all she got in return was denial, rationalization, and stonewalling. He was a deeply insecure person, inwardly terrified of being questioned and having his weaknesses exposed. Further communication with him only added more insult to injury. Even the intervention of impartial third parties did no good. The two of them were at a complete impasse.

Jennifer's anger was quickly turning into long-term resentment and bitterness. Overwhelmed by it all, she didn't know what to do. How was she going to resolve this tidal wave of negative emotion that had crashed over her, rolling her over and over? Revenge was certainly the easiest option to contemplate. Fantasies of how it might be done came naturally to her imagination. But Jennifer was a deeply devoted follower of Jesus and knew that forgiveness was the option she must choose. It was the Christ-like thing to do. Moreover, she was so tired of thinking about him and realized that her unforgiveness was only hurting herself. She decided to forgive him and move on.

But Jennifer discovered that she simply could not, no matter how hard she tried. Although she had the will to forgive him, her negative thoughts and feelings toward him remained strong. They continued to pop up into her consciousness, whenever her attention was not focused on something else. They were relentless, intrusive, and sometimes even homicidal. She could find no peace from them.

Desperate for help, Jennifer turned to her pastor, who led her through an eloquent prayer, declaring her forgiveness toward the person who had injured her. As they prayed together, she felt a genuine sense of release, her anger subsiding. She thought she had finally forgiven him, but days later to her disappointment, her unforgiving thoughts returned. She continued to pray about it both by herself and with other people. And although more prayer helped, it was never enough to fully set her free. Feeling discouraged and tormented by her own mind, Jennifer wondered what she was doing wrong. The best she could do was repress her unforgiveness and pretend that it wasn't there. But during moments when she was honest with herself, she had to admit that her resentment remained and was draining much of her energy.

Jennifer's inability to fully forgive was not due to lack of either choice or faith, as some of those around her insensitively suggested, but the result of a deep inner conflict. As much as a part of her really wanted to forgive and forget, another did not. Whenever she imagined saying the words *I forgive you* to him, this other part of her didn't believe what she was saying. It defiantly refused to forgive, vehemently voicing its objection in the form of a rhetorical question: *How can I accept the unacceptable?* I call this inward resistance to forgive, the *Acceptance Conundrum*.

In Greek mythology, the Sphinx was a creature with a human head and the body of a lion who guarded the entrance to the ancient City of Thebes. Travelers were not allowed to pass unless they could solve its riddle. Those who could not, it devoured. Likewise, unforgiveness will eat us alive unless we can get through it. The Acceptance Conundrum is the riddle of this inner psychological Sphinx, blocking our path to deep forgiveness until we can provide an acceptable answer.

Many cases of unforgiveness are as difficult as Jennifer's. They exhibit the common pattern of trying hard to forgive but not succeeding, not understanding why, and then settling for unsteady unsustainable repression. They may display symptoms such as anxiety, depression, numbness, insomnia, headaches, rage, obsessive thoughts, spiritual deadness, and Post-Traumatic Stress Disorder (PTSD). There can even be physical consequences as serious as lower immunity to cancer.

A 2019 research study by the Barna Group found that one in four practicing Christians struggles to forgive someone. When we find ourselves similarly stuck, struggling to forgive those who have wronged us badly, how can we make progress? And even in cases not as severe, how do we resolve those lingering strands of resentment keeping us from the complete inner peace we seek?

In this book, we will learn how we can move forward more speedily on our path to deep forgiveness by examining the language we use to define and speak forgiveness. We will explore the two core pillars of forgiveness and discover why they are often so difficult to do. Most importantly, we will find a way to solve the riddle of the Acceptance Conundrum, this subtle and profound obstacle to full forgiveness freedom. Jennifer will continue to be with us on this journey. We will see how the insights ahead have helped her to find inner peace.

1. THE SIGNIFICANCE OF LANGUAGE

The language we use to define and speak forgiveness affects how well we can forgive. The specific words and sentences we use matter; some are far more effective than others. In this chapter, you will discover how to speak forgiveness in a manner which penetrates your own heart. By learning the language of deep forgiveness, you will be able to forgive more quickly and deeply, finding the peace and freedom you seek more readily.

Let's begin with an exercise to uncover the particular language you have been using to forgive:

Exercise: Speaking Forgiveness in Your Mind
1. Think of someone you need to forgive more deeply.
2. As vividly as you can, imagine the offender in the room in front of you, picturing their facial expression, posture, and clothing.
3. Write down in one or two sentences how you would speak forgiveness to them, only in your mind, not necessarily what you would want to say directly.
4. Speak (out loud if possible) forgiveness to this person

using what you wrote.

5. Notice any change in your feelings toward them.

6. Rate how much you have forgiven the offender on a scale of 1 to 10, with 1 indicating no forgiveness, and 10 indicating complete forgiveness. Write down this number; it is your forgiveness rating for this person.

Did the exercise produce any effect on your feelings toward the offender? If the impact you experienced was significant, that is certainly good news. But if it was not, you need not be discouraged because help is on the way in this book. Regardless of the outcome of the exercise, your forgiveness language can likely be improved to have greater effect.

The statement you spontaneously constructed reflects how you naturally understand forgiveness, the learning you obtained from a variety of sources: dictionaries, teachers, and living with others in community, especially family and church. Dictionaries, both secular and theological, are very limited in defining forgiveness in a way that is practically useful. Some are even harmfully unrealistic and idealistic. (See the Appendix for examples and discussion.) Spiritual teachers have developed various prayer models to help us forgive. You may have adopted some of their language as your own. One such example is:

"Father God, in the name of Jesus Christ, I choose to forgive (the offender) for (the offense). Forgive me for my bitterness toward (the offender). I confess and repent of this sin, and nail it to the cross of Jesus. I choose to release it completely to You."

These kinds of prayers, which declare one's forgiveness toward an offender, can be spiritually powerful by asserting the theological basis for forgiveness to proceed forward. But yet in many instances, they seem insufficient to complete the process. After praying these prayers, some forgivers experience initial relief only to later find their unforgiving thoughts returning, requiring them to pray the same prayers again and again. Have you also experienced this need for repetition in your own prayers or in speaking forgiveness to someone in your mind? Something is clearly missing in the way we forgive, especially in cases in which the injury is severe and the resentment resilient.

That something, crucial to forgiveness, missing from most prayer models and dictionary definitions of forgiveness, is **language that speaks to the heart in terms that the heart can hear.** Your understanding of how to define and speak forgiveness has been derived from limited or inadequate resources, which we will now remedy.

Let's consider as an alternative this practical conversational definition of forgiveness, which contains two pillars or core attitudes, expressed by Statements, A and B:

Forgiveness is having an attitude toward the offender which both states:

A. "You don't have to make up for what you did to me."

B. "I don't have to hurt you for hurting me."

Picture in your mind the word, "FORGIVENESS," written on a crossbeam, supported by two pillars, one marked "A" and the other "B". Forgiveness, represented by the crossbeam, is held up by its two core attitudes, the pillars. Pillar A lets go of the demand for restitution, while Pillar B lets go of the demand for retribution. This metaphor of *the Two Pillars* will be used throughout this book to organize and structure our understanding of forgiveness.

Think of the particular Statements, A and B, above, as one view of the Two Pillars, which we will refer to as the Basic View. Eventually, we will develop a total of four distinct views, using slightly different Statements to express the same core attitudes of the pillars from a variety of important perspectives. In the last chapter, we will build a full detailed description of our forgiveness metaphor using everything we will learn.

Now let's do our speaking exercise again using the Basic View.

Exercise: Speaking Deep Forgiveness in Your Mind
1. Think of someone you need to forgive more deeply.
2. As vividly as you can, imagine the offender in the room in front of you, picturing their facial expression, posture, and clothing.
3. Speak (out loud if possible) forgiveness to this person

using Statement A:

A. "You don't have to make up for what you did to me."

Repeat this several times, pausing for a moment after each time to notice how you feel before continuing.

4. Speak (out loud if possible) forgiveness to this person using Statement B:

B. "I don't have to hurt you for hurting me."

Repeat this several times, as before.

5. Notice any change in your feelings toward them.

6. On a scale of 1 to 10, rate how much you have forgiven the offender, with 1 indicating no forgiveness, and 10 indicating complete forgiveness. Write it down.

How did you feel after doing the exercise this time? You might have experienced some resistance, relief, or resolution. Resistance would reveal that there is a pillar of forgiveness that is hard for you to accept. Relief would mean that your heart has finally been able to hear forgiveness spoken with words that it can understand. Resolution would indicate that you have been ready to forgive for a long time and just needed the right words to solidify it.

Did you experience any difference between this exercise and the previous one? How much did your forgiveness rating change? It is likely you felt more emotional impact doing this later exercise because of the differences in the language used. When Jennifer participated in the exercise, she exclaimed in surprise, "It really does make a difference!" Using this new forgiveness language felt more genuine to her, reaching a much deeper place in her heart.

Forgiveness speaks primarily to the heart, especially your own heart. When you declare your forgiveness, above all others, you are speaking your intent to *yourself*. You are communicating the forgiving attitudes you wish your heart to adopt. **It is not necessary and often unwise for you to speak directly to the offender, who may not appreciate your forgiveness.** Regardless of whether the offender, others, or God hear your words, it is *your own heart* that matters the most for you to gain freedom from unforgiveness.

To forgive well, you must use language that your heart can receive and comprehend, language that is simple, concrete, direct, child-like, and conversational. This natural language of your emotional center uses experiential terms which even a young child can understand. Young children generally do not understand theological concepts such as "the cross of Jesus." If your language is too abstract, your heart will have a hard time hearing it.

Did you experience any difference between speaking the two Statements in this exercise? If you noticed some difference in your emotional response, it's because the Two Pillars are independent processes; they function each on their own. One woman realized that she was able to let go of her demand for retribution, but still struggled very much with restitution. This discovery helped her to focus in on what specific work remained to forgive more completely in her heart.

Forgiveness joins together these two distinct psychological processes of the pillars. Each one needs to be addressed and practiced separately, and then be united with the other to form a complete whole. Only after you have practiced well having each attitude toward the offender will you know what you mean when you say, *I forgive*. Otherwise, simply saying those words without deeper understanding will do little for your heart. Once practiced, both processes may be effectively considered a single concept using the word *forgive*. When done well, they produce a desirable emotional release, the natural letting go of anger, bitterness, and resentment.

Practicing Deep Forgiveness

Speaking forgiveness powerfully requires more than just the right words and sentences themselves; it also depends on the way in which they are spoken. In other words, *It's not just what you say, but how you say it.* The energy in your voice matters, as well as your intonation as you pronounce each word. Even your posture and gestures contribute to a full-person experience in which your body language and vocal tone match what you are saying. The practice of speaking forgiveness is most effective when you put your whole self into it. This can be done just in your mind or out loud, by yourself or with others. It does not have to be spoken to the offender directly.

A good strategy to learn a complex skill is to break it down into simpler parts, practice each part separately until proficient, and then combine the parts together. This strategy works well in almost all fields of performance training, from music to gymnastics to mathematics.

One of my favorite hobbies is playing the guitar, which involves the coordination of my left and right hands. With my left hand, I have to produce the correct fingering of chords on the fretboard, while with my right, I have to strum the right strings at the right time in right rhythm. When I was first learning to play guitar, it was very difficult to do both at the same time. If I focused more on my left hand chord fingering, my right hand would fall out of rhythm, causing me to lose my timing in the song. If I paid more attention to my strumming, my left hand would finger the strings in the wrong place, producing an unpleasant discordant sound. My skills didn't improve very much until I started practicing them individually.

By focusing only on changing chords, my fingerings became quick and precise, and so well practiced that I didn't have to think about the placement of particular fingers anymore. And by giving my sole attention to playing different strumming patterns, I was able make the process of changing patterns while staying on meter so automatic that I didn't have to think about each strum anymore. The final step was to put the two skills together and coordinate them, which was much easier after practicing them individually. I had to practice, practice, and practice them together until I no longer had to concentrate on the playing, but only sense the flow of the music. At times I played so intuitively with such wholehearted engagement that I felt at one with the music, the experience of being in the musician's groove.

Of course, learning to forgive is much more complex than learning to play the guitar, but some principles may apply to both, such as individual focus, repetitive practice, and being fully engaged. By focusing on each pillar of forgiveness individually, you can identify which one, if any, is troubling you. Then you can try to uncover the source of the resistance and address the issues causing it. If you are having a hard time forgiving someone, ask yourself which pillar is more difficult to say? Considering each situation individually may reveal to you what issues you need to address: Perhaps the first pillar is hard because you are still grieving the loss caused by this person? Or perhaps the other is difficult because you still desire revenge?

Repetitive practice is necessary and good when done in moderation. Saying that you forgive once and then trying to forget is surely not enough, while saying it a thousand times a day is certainly too much. My suggestion is that whenever unforgiving thoughts arise, address them with the pillar which most applies at that moment and then turn your attention elsewhere. Don't completely ignore the thoughts, but don't dwell on them either. Be aware that repetitive practice alone is often not sufficient to complete the process, so avoid getting frustrated by over-practicing. If my guitar was mistuned or had a broken string, my playing would sound awful regardless of how much I practiced. It would need tuning or repairs. Likewise, when practicing forgiveness has reached a plateau, additional insights which we will discover ahead, will be needed to make the process more effective.

Being fully engaged means committing all the necessary mental resources to the forgiveness task at hand. Be receptive to your inner thoughts and feelings. Take time to reflect on them and let your intuition guide you. Try speaking the pillars of forgiveness out loud. Hearing yourself through your ears creates new neurological pathways which deepen the impact of those statements in your mind; you hear not only your words, but the tone and emotion in your voice too, creating a fuller experience. Keep in mind that choice and commitment are only the beginning of the process. It will take time for you to develop the inner awareness and understanding necessary to complete the journey.

Jennifer made very little progress in forgiving her abuser by simply repeating, *I forgive you,* in her head. But when she started using the language of deep forgiveness, her ability to forgive improved. These particular words touched her heart more deeply and enabled her to practice individually each pillar. Although she still had a long road ahead, Jennifer felt relieved that she was finally making some significant progress.

In the next chapter, we will explore the origin of the Two Pillars of forgiveness.

2. TWO NATURAL LAWS

The two distinct pillars of forgiveness address two natural psychological laws of social justice, the Laws of Restitution and Retribution. These laws have been written into the DNA of the human soul, heart and mind, instinctively known by children without having to be taught. No child needs instruction on the rules of *Gimme back what you took from me!* and *If you hit me, I'm gonna hit you back harder!* They become aware of them just fine on their own.

Every culture has its own manifestation of the Natural Laws. In the U. S. and elsewhere, how many revenge movies are produced every year? The number is seemingly endless. Even the most forgiving of us, can't help but delight in the moment when evil characters get what they deserve in the end. Movies are just fantasy entertainment, but in unguarded moments they reveal what is lurking in the human psyche.

The Law of Restitution is a demand for fair repayment or compensation. It can be stated in many ways including:

> *They must make up for what they did to me;*
> *They must pay the debt they owe me;*

They must repair the harm they caused me.

The Law of Retribution is a demand for just punishment or consequences. It can be stated in many ways including:

I must hurt them for hurting me;
They must be punished for their offense;
An eye for an eye;
A tooth for a tooth.

The ancient Roman legal principle of *lex talionis* placed restrictions on revenge so that "an eye for an eye" meant ONLY an eye for an eye, prohibiting the taking of two eyes for an eye. When unchecked, the human psyche has a tendency to take punishment too far.

Far older than Roman culture, biblical mandates arising from the Natural Laws are found together in the Book of Leviticus in which God speaks to Moses:

'Anyone who takes the life of a human being is to be put to death. Anyone who takes the life of someone's animal must make restitution—life for life. Anyone who injures their neighbor is to be injured in the same manner: fracture for fracture, eye for eye, tooth for tooth. The one who has inflicted the injury must suffer the same injury. Whoever kills an animal must make restitution, but whoever kills a human being is to be put to death. You are to have the same law for the foreigner and the

native-born. I am the LORD your God.' (Leviticus 24:20–
22)

The laws of the psyche were made into explicit societal laws
to provide for orderly justice and prevent uncontrolled
vengeance.[1]

Moreover, the Natural Laws can be expressed in three levels:
personal, societal, and universal. Enforcement at the personal
level between individuals, also known as "taking the law into
your own hands" or "frontier justice," often happens, even
though personal revenge is clearly prohibited by biblical law
(Lev 19:18). Enforcement at the societal level of the laws of the
State are handled by the police and the courts. Enforcement at
the universal level is the divine prerogative; final justice is
God's responsibility. In particular situations, the responsible
authority at each level can choose to set aside or nullify the law,
making it void and unenforced.

Forgiveness is the setting aside of these Natural Laws. At the
personal level, forgiveness is an individual choice; we are given
the freewill either to forgive or not forgive. At the societal level,
forgiveness is occasionally done by executive pardon or judicial
ruling. At the universal level, the atoning work of Christ on our
behalf makes the full forgiveness of God possible. At each level,
the responsible authority chooses whether or not to forgive.

On a grassy hillside, overlooking the Sea of Galilee, Jesus
gave his famous Sermon on the Mount, in which he taught his
disciples to set aside the Law of Restitution at the personal level,

modeling to them how to pray: "And forgive us our debts, as we also have forgiven our debtors." (Matt 6:12) In this, his Lord's prayer, "our debts" are what we owe in restitution, and "our debtors" are those who owe us restitution. We are to forgive those who have sinned against us, even when they haven't made amends.

Jesus also taught his followers to set aside the Law of Retribution at the personal level: "You have heard that it was said, 'An eye for an eye, and a tooth for a tooth.' But now I tell you: do not take revenge on someone who wrongs you. If anyone slaps you on the right cheek, let him slap your left cheek too." (Matt 5:38–39, GNT) A slap on the cheek by the back of the hand at this time was considered a great insult, the equivalent of a certain well-known gesture by the middle finger today. We are to refrain from revenge and not be easily provoked into striking back.

Jesus shows us the meaning of personal forgiveness, but it can still be very hard to emulate. It can often seem impossible to set aside laws so deeply embedded into the psyche. Bitterness, resentment, and violation are not easily transformed. Patterns of unforgiving thoughts are resistant to change. It takes time, repetition, awareness and deep reflection for forgiveness to travel fully to the depths of both mind and heart. This can be a difficult process.

The root meaning of biblical forgiveness is enlightening. In New Testament Greek, the word for forgiveness is *aphesis*. Its underlying meaning contains several nuances, including "to let go," and "to let be."[2] These different shades of meaning inform us regarding how forgiveness works in different situations. Here we will focus on the significance of *letting go*. In the next chapter, we will discuss the importance of *letting be*.

Forgiveness is the *letting go* of our demand for these laws to be enforced. We can practice doing this with these affirmations:

A. "I choose to set aside the **Law of Restitution** at the personal level and let go of my demand that it be enforced."

B. "I choose to set aside the **Law of Retribution** at the personal level and let go of my demand that it be enforced."

These statements express the Legal View of our Two Pillars. This view is more conceptually abstract, providing the legal basis for personal forgiveness to occur while communicating a language of deep forgiveness for the philosophical mind to comprehend.

Let's consider a hypothetical scenario in which some people damage your property, such as crashing their car through a wall of your house. Should they pay for your repairs, which would be considered an act of restitution? If they don't volunteer to do so, should you ask them to pay? Or are you prohibited from asking since you consider yourself a forgiving person who just set aside the Law of Restitution and doesn't want to be a hypocrite? Take a moment to think about this before continuing.

Letting go of the Law of Restitution doesn't mean that restitution shouldn't be made. If someone damages your property, they should pay for repairs if they can. It would be the right thing to do. You can ask for a payment, but if they can't or won't, you will need to go through the process of forgiving them. The difference is in the degree of demand, and the ability to let go of it.

A helpful distinction to make is between laws and principles. Laws are rigid and *must* be followed, as in the saying, "The law is the law, no exceptions!" In contrast, principles are flexible and *should* be followed, as we might say, "In principle, we do things a certain way, but we can make an exception in this case." The principle of restitution can be kept while setting aside the law. We can apply the principle without being bound by the law. We can seek restitution but can also choose to let it go and accept the situation when necessary.

Suppose those who damage your property initially refuse to pay. And it is not worth it for you to take them to civil court, so you decide to forgive them. But later they feel guilty and send you a check to cover your damages. One day, you get your mail and are surprised to find their payment in your hands. Should you deposit that check, even though you have already forgiven them? Take a moment to think about this before continuing.

You can accept their payment because although you have let go of your *demand* for restitution, you can still *want* them to do the right thing. Although you have accepted their refusal to pay, you can still *wish* that they choose to pay you. Even if you had spoken to them directly and released them from the legal obligation to pay, that would not have changed the intrinsic rightness of them making restitution. **The moral responsibility to do what is right always remains**. Forgiveness does not take it away; the moral universe does not change. If you forgive someone for stealing from you, they still have a moral calling to return what they have stolen, even if you have moved on and no longer expect it back.

Now let's consider the Law of Retribution in the car crash scenario. Suppose you learn that the accident was not due to mechanical failure, but to them being drunk. By forgiving them, you have set aside the Law of Retribution at the personal level and let go of your *demand* for retribution. However, in principle, you can still *want* them to experience consequences for their behavior which teach them to be more responsible, possibly preventing harm to others in the future. You can still *wish* that the state authorities penalize them for their reckless behavior. But if the government decides not to prosecute or the court's verdict is flawed, you have to be able to accept it, otherwise, you have not really forgiven them.

When our demands against offenders are left unmet, frustration builds inside of us and hardens into bitterness. Hanging on to such demands for long can only continue to hurt us, inevitably becoming destructive to our souls. But by turning them into wishes, we instead gain inner peace, mental freedom, and healing for ourselves.

The concepts in this chapter helped Jennifer understand that it was okay for her to feel and acknowledge the power of the Natural Laws residing in her heart. They gave her permission to be genuine regarding her desires for restitution and retribution. Jennifer can still *want* both, as long as her psyche was not bound by her *demand* for it. She can still *wish* for some kind of compensation for the harm she suffered, even though complete restitution for her was impossible. She can still *wish* that some kind of corrective action be taken, while deferring its form entirely to God. This all made forgiveness seem more achievable to her. Forgiveness does not prohibit our natural desires for restitution and retribution, as long as we can fully accept not having them fulfilled, as long as our hearts are not consumed by them. With God's help, they can be reduced over time to the point of being barely noticeable or even zero in some cases, no longer affecting our inner peace.

In the next chapter, we will see in detail how forgiveness relates to the concept of acceptance.

3. THE ACCEPTANCE CONUNDRUM

Forgiveness is a kind of acceptance, as a rose is a kind of flower. To forgive is to also accept, to let be; the other of its important nuances from the previous chapter. Acceptance is desirable; it is peace and rest for tired souls. Yet something indignant inside us can quickly arise in protest: *But wait, how can I accept the unacceptable? I am so right and so deserve complete vindication. They are so wrong and so deserve to suffer the consequences of their injustice. How can I possibly accept anything less? This is just unacceptable!* This thought process expresses the Acceptance Conundrum, a deep tension impairing our ability to forgive, unless we find a way to release it. We will discover such a means of resolution by understanding two special forms of acceptance: *existential* and *moral*. They reveal to us how to accept offenders without accepting their character.

First, let's begin by defining two terms: *existential acceptance* and *existential rejection*. The word *existential* may seem like an abstract, hard-to-understand philosophical concept, but it really is quite simple and essential once we learn it. It is an adjective that means "regarding what exists or what is." It simply informs us that we are talking about the concept of existence.

Have you ever seen the Milky Way with your naked eye? Out in the desert, away from city lights, a breathtaking band of diffuse white light can be seen stretching across the nighttime sky. Having the appearance of spilt milk, this cosmic glow is actually the collective light emitted from over 100 billion stars in our galaxy, each one too far away for our eyes to see individually without the aid of a telescope. The known universe contains over 100 billion galaxies, spread out over all space and time as interconnected, crisscrossing strands of faint distant light, resembling a spider web of unimaginable immensity. This is our astronomical picture of the Existence of Everything. Thinking about it makes us feel so very small.

Have you ever wondered why there is something instead of nothing? Existence didn't have to exist. There could have been just nothingness. But God had a purpose, most of which is still quite mysterious. He chose to create the universe for this reason; and so here we are; here we find ourselves existing, needing to find meaning for existing.

Have you ever pondered the mystery of your own existence? You did not choose the time and place of your birth. You did not choose your parents, family, culture, and genetics. Why are you … *you*, and not someone else? We all exist with the sense of having been individually thrown into existence from somewhere else for reasons unfathomable, out of our control. And here we find ourselves, perplexed and humbled, accidents of birth, living the given lives we must accept.

3. The Acceptance Conundrum

Existence is fundamentally mysterious; and its mystery surrounds us. Our everyday concerns distract us from our awareness of it; but it is always there, always present. This brief moment of reflection draws us into an *experience* of what *existential* means and will deepen our understanding of its usage ahead. Let's continue on to define important additional words and terms.

The basic definition of *acceptance* is "the act of consenting to receive." This is the most general and familiar form of acceptance, which we use to acknowledge our acceptance of such everyday things as gifts, packages, job offers, and friendships.

Existential acceptance is accepting the existence of something, as it is. We can say, "It is what it is," to communicate our acceptance of an unpleasant situation that we don't want to be true. Regarding difficult people, we can say, "They are who they are," or, "That's just the way they are." To an offender, we might say, "I tolerate your existence, although you make it very hard to do so." For example, those of us who had difficult parents may arrive at a point of existential acceptance, realizing that they did what they could for us, as imperfect as they were. Existential acceptance in our hearts produces feelings of calm, peace, tolerance, and contentment. But it is not passivity. We can want others to change, but we do not demand it, respecting their freedom, rights and personal boundaries. We can try hard to make the world a better place, but at the same time we let go of our demand for existence to be anything other than it is. We turn over our attachment to the outcome of our efforts to God. We accept that the past cannot be changed.

Existential rejection (or *non-acceptance*) is the opposite of *existential acceptance.* It is rejecting the existence of something, as it is. When we reject or can't accept news of a shocking personal tragedy, we might say, "It just can't be true!" or, "Tell me it isn't so!" This commonly happens in the stage of grief known as denial. Regarding people who turn out to be shockingly bad, we might exclaim, "They can't be this bad!" Toward a personal offender, we might think, *The world would be a better place without you,* or *I can have peace only when you are gone,* or *How could a terrible person like you be allowed to exist?* or even, *I'd like to push you off a cliff!* Indeed, it is the murder of another in our hearts or in some cases in reality. Sadly, the daily news is an unending torrent of such examples of cruelty, hatred, and exploitation. We feel the symptoms of existential rejection: regret, resentment, restlessness, and discontentment. We demand that others change to suit ourselves without respect for their rights and personal boundaries. To reject the existence of others, as they are, is to need them to either be different or die, the essence of playing God as the Judge of Existence.

A deep connection exists between forgiveness and existential acceptance, and between unforgiveness and existential rejection. The basis of forgiveness is existential acceptance; for it is impossible to forgive others when we can't tolerate their existence. And the essence of unforgiveness is existential rejection; for the desire to destroy another's existence springs out of not being able to forgive.

Next, let's continue by defining the terms: *moral acceptance* and *moral rejection*. The word *moral* means "concerning what is right or should be." It is an adjective regarding ethical values, choices, and judgments of right or wrong, good or evil. It simply informs us that we are talking about what is right or wrong.

Moral acceptance is judging that something has good or good enough values. We might say, "It is as it should be," or, "They are as they should be." Toward an offender, we might say, "You're not so bad; you didn't intend any harm." For example, this is something we might say to a friend who had good intentions to help but said some wrong and offensive things to us instead.

Moral rejection (or *non-acceptance*) is the opposite of *moral acceptance*. We might protest, "It should not be that way!" or, "They should not be that way!" Toward an offender, we might say, "I reject your values, choices, and character," or more simply, "You're so wrong!" These statements can express our moral rejection and revulsion of such things as corrupt institutions, hypocritical leaders, and bullies.

Let's take a moment to relax and review what we have just accomplished. We have defined two special forms of acceptance: *existential* and *moral*. Toward any particular situation or person, we can choose to either *accept* or *reject* (not accept) each form. This gives us the four possible attitudes we can take: existential acceptance, existential rejection, moral acceptance, and moral rejection. Two of these choices, existential acceptance and moral rejection, will be particularly helpful in deepening our ability to forgive; let's see how.

The Acceptance Conundrum is caused by unclear thinking, by the confusion of not knowing which form of acceptance is meant in our thoughts. Consider the simple statement, "I accept them." What does the word *accept* mean here? Does it refer to existential acceptance, moral acceptance, or both? Or could it refer to neither, but instead only to the general form of acceptance? Its meaning is ambiguous without more context for interpretation.

Now consider again the question: *How can I accept the unacceptable?* Without the deeper understanding of the two special forms of acceptance, this question contains a contradiction. It is similar to asking, "How can I do something (*accept*) that I cannot do (*the unacceptable*)?" Of course, the question appears unanswerable. I am being asked to do the impossible. I can't do it. But then how do I forgive? I can't do what I must do, which means I have to do the impossible! Now this is a conundrum!

Our perplexing predicament is resolved by realizing that the word *accept* and the term *the unacceptable* can refer to two different forms of acceptance. We can accept the unacceptable if *accept* is used in the existential sense and *the unacceptable* is used in the moral sense. We can accept others' existence without accepting their moral character. And *this* is what forgiveness asks of us.

3. The Acceptance Conundrum

This way of thinking can be clarified using a simple analogy with ice cream. Can you like ice cream and not like ice cream? You can't do both because they represent a contradiction. You can't do something and its opposite at the same time. Can you like chocolate ice cream and not like vanilla ice cream? Now you can do both because you are distinguishing between two kinds of ice cream. In the same way, you can accept the unacceptable by distinguishing between two kinds of acceptance: You can accept the existence of the offender and not the moral values, character, or behavior of the person. Or you can *existentially* accept the offender and not *morally* accept the person. Or you can *existentially* accept the *morally* unacceptable. These are three ways of saying the same thing. It is essentially as easy as liking one kind of ice cream and not the other.

If we did not know about the two special forms of acceptance, our thinking would have been more rigid and limited, confounding the *existential* with the *moral*. We would not be able to resolve the Acceptance Conundrum and the underlying cognitive tension would have simply remained as an obstacle to full forgiveness. It would be a tight psychological Gordian knot buried deep within the neural structures of our brains.

Let's try out our new flexible way of thinking on the most despicable dictator from human history who comes to your mind right now. You can say that "Despicable Dictator" is *existentially acceptable*, even though he is *morally unacceptable*. This dictator is existentially acceptable because he is existentially acceptable to God, otherwise the Creator would have ended his existence or caused him to never have been born. If we trust God's wisdom, then we must also accept this person having existed. Our affirmation of his moral unacceptability makes this easier by balancing out our thought process between the two special forms of acceptance. This way of speaking about acceptance will help you to begin to forgive him, even as despicable as he is. However, unless you have been directly affected by him, your feelings toward him may be mild. If so, consider this merely a practice run.

When existential acceptance is especially difficult toward someone you truly despise, it may help to break the process down into four simple steps, saying to yourself the following statements, meditating on each point before moving on:

1. "I trust the wisdom of God."
2. "God accepts the offender's existence."
3. "Therefore, I must also accept their existence."
4. "I existentially accept the morally unacceptable."

Existential acceptance is ultimately an act of deepest faith in God.

Now let's look at Jesus' beloved Parable of the Prodigal Son, which illustrates well the importance of knowing how to resolve the Acceptance Conundrum.

Jesus continued: "There was a man who had two

3. The Acceptance Conundrum

sons. The younger one said to his father, 'Father, give me my share of the estate.' So he divided his property between them. Not long after that, the younger son got together all he had, set off for a distant country and there squandered his wealth in wild living. After he had spent everything, there was a severe famine in that whole country, and he began to be in need. So he went and hired himself out to a citizen of that country, who sent him to his fields to feed pigs. He longed to fill his stomach with the pods that the pigs were eating, but no one gave him anything. When he came to his senses, he said, 'How many of my father's hired servants have food to spare, and here I am starving to death! I will set out and go back to my father and say to him: Father, I have sinned against heaven and against you. I am no longer worthy to be called your son; make me like one of your hired servants.' So he got up and went to his father.

But while he was still a long way off, his father saw him and was filled with compassion for him; he ran to his son, threw his arms around him and kissed him. The son said to him, 'Father, I have sinned against heaven and against you. I am no longer worthy to be called your son.' But the father said to his servants, 'Quick! Bring the best robe and put it on him. Put a ring on his finger and sandals on his feet. Bring the fattened calf and kill it. Let's have a feast and celebrate. For this son of mine was dead and is alive again; he was lost and is found.' So they

35

began to celebrate.

Meanwhile, the older son was in the field. When he came near the house, he heard music and dancing. So he called one of the servants and asked him what was going on. 'Your brother has come,' he replied, 'and your father has killed the fattened calf because he has him back safe and sound.' The older brother became angry and refused to go in. So his father went out and pleaded with him. But he answered his father, 'Look! All these years I've been slaving for you and never disobeyed your orders. Yet you never gave me even a young goat so I could celebrate with my friends. But when this son of yours who has squandered your property with prostitutes comes home, you kill the fattened calf for him!' 'My son,' the father said, 'you are always with me, and everything I have is yours. But we had to celebrate and be glad, because this brother of yours was dead and is alive again; he was lost and is found.' (Luke 15:11–32)

The father and the older son could not be more different in their reaction to the younger son's return. The younger son, by his own admission, had greatly sinned against God and his father. Upon hearing his confession, his father did not rebuke him, which would have communicated his acknowledgement that his son had been indeed *morally unacceptable*. You see, to the father, his son was also *existentially acceptable*, whom he still recognized as his own. The father rejoiced that his son was alive

3. The Acceptance Conundrum

and still existing. He existentially accepted his morally unacceptable son and forgave him.

In contrast, the older son held great resentment toward his brother. We can imagine what went through his mind upon hearing of his brother's return, *What? He's back! How dare he come back after abandoning us. I've had to labor twice as hard for years ever since he left! It's all his fault! I can't stand the sight of him. I wish he were dead. He's no brother of mine!* The older son had been deeply hurt by his brother's leaving, experiencing it as a personal betrayal. And now, standing outside the house, with his long-lost brother inside, he just couldn't bring himself to come in. A part of him may have wanted to forgive, but a stronger part refused. He could not resolve his Acceptance Conundrum; he could not accept the unacceptable. He viewed his brother as wholly unacceptable, lumping together the existential and the moral. Unable to forgive, he could only refer to him as "this son of yours," rejecting his brother's existence as his brother.

We experience the Acceptance Conundrum most intensely toward those who have severely betrayed our trust. These people are of course the hardest to forgive. Toward most other offenders we may only feel the tension in subtle ways, manifesting as a slight mental discomfort or a vague feeling that something doesn't quite make sense. Whatever our present situation, having learned the distinction between existential and moral acceptance, we are prepared to recognize and overcome this obstacle to forgiveness whenever it appears.

This understanding helped Jennifer to move beyond her struggle with the Acceptance Conundrum. Now, whenever she found herself asking, *How can I accept the unacceptable?*, she knew how to answer. Eventually, the question faded completely from her mind, allowing her to forgive more deeply.

Jesus himself was the ultimate master at existentially accepting the morally unacceptable. He was known for eating and drinking with sinners, welcoming and befriending them (Luke 5:30, 7:34, 15:2). But accepting their friendship did not mean he would look the other way regarding their character. To a woman caught in adultery facing the death penalty, he said, "Neither do I condemn you. Go now and leave your life of sin." (John 8:11) He wanted her to continue to exist, but to live a morally better life. His attitude and words to her demonstrate to us how to live a forgiving life.

The foundation of forgiveness is existentially accepting the morally unacceptable. Simply repeating and meditating on this statement will help you forgive more easily by training your mind to naturally separate the two special forms of acceptance. But the solution to the Acceptance Conundrum does more than just support forgiveness. It applies not only to those who have injured us, but moves beyond to everyone else, to all of humanity. It is a way of living with divine insight, of being in the world and seeing others through spiritually enlightened eyes.

Our understanding of how to resolve the Acceptance Conundrum can also help us make our definition of forgiveness more powerful and complete. Following Jesus' example above, we can refine our Two Pillars by adding a moral clause to the beginning of each statement, creating the Expanded View:

Forgiveness is having an attitude toward the offender which both states:

A. "Although it would be the right thing to do, you don't have to make up for what you did to me."
B. "Although it would be a fair thing to do, I don't have to hurt you for hurting me."

In the first Statement, we *existentially accept* the offender as being unable or unwilling to make restitution. We recognize that this is not a person who takes responsibility to make up for the harm they cause, whether partially or completely if possible. We choose to let go of a demand that is emotionally detrimental to hang on to any longer. However, the additional clause makes clear that our existential acceptance in no way diminishes our moral stance regarding what is right, often in direct opposition to the attitude of the offender.

In the second, our existential acceptance of the offender allows us to let go of our demand for retribution for the sake of personal freedom and higher spiritual values. Here, the additional clause makes clear that our existential acceptance in no way reduces the seriousness of the injury or the fairness of our moral instinct, calling out for a reciprocal response.

The Expanded View emphasizes together both existential

acceptance and moral rejection (non-acceptance) toward the offender. Its balanced language relieves the discomfort which occurs when either side appears to dominate over the other in our thinking. It makes Statements, A and B, more palatable and agreeable to heart and mind. This is an important step in the direction of "loving the sinner while hating the sin."

Jennifer discovered that the Expanded View enabled her to forgive more deeply by implicitly alleviating her distress with the Acceptance Conundrum. Her heart was able to receive this expression of the Two Pillars at a much deeper level. Those like her also found this view very helpful, while some others preferred the simplicity of the Basic View.

We can give our definition of forgiveness a different emotional impact by rewriting it to explicitly emphasize acceptance, using the word *accept*. Acceptance was always inherent in our definition, but here we clearly specify it:

Forgiveness is having an attitude toward the offender which both states:
   A. "I accept that you will never make up for what you did to me, although it would be the right thing to do."
   B. "I accept that I will never hurt you for hurting me, although it would be a fair thing to do."

Let's call this the Full View of our definition of forgiveness. The words *accept* and *never* are powerful words, which carry much added emotional impact when stated explicitly. Our latest view uses a more receptive voice, and conveys a greater sense of finality, a last letting go, a final giving up. For many, including Jennifer, this view was more difficult to say and mean, because it penetrated even deeper into the heart, encountering the hardest layers of resistance. By addressing the future, as well as the present, this view utilizes the strongest language needed to forgive with the full acceptance required to heal the deepest wounds.

Even so, the struggle to get to that place in the heart can feel like a war within. To be against something is to oppose it. To be against someone is to fight them. So, to give up our demands against the offender can feel like surrender, a form of losing we disdain. No one wants to give their ground, lose the battle, or admit defeat. But instead of hanging on to false hope, we can win by realizing that when we forgive, we surrender not to our adversaries, but to God. We surrender our wills to accept Existence as God accepts it, to existentially accept the morally unacceptable, as he does. This is the paradoxical surrender that leads to spiritual victory.

So far, we have created four essentially equivalent views of our definition of forgiveness: Legal, Basic, Expanded, and Full. Practice using the ones which impact you the most, those which generate feelings of resistance, relief, or resolution. Try to notice the subtle differences in how you respond to each one, each having its own distinctive value to your soul. Use them to address any unforgiving thoughts toward the offender that appear.

If you find yourself especially troubled by obsessive unforgiving thoughts, you can gently disrupt them by using the E.A.T.M.U. Method. E.A.T.M.U. stands for *Existentially Accepting The Morally Unacceptable*. We can represent this concept by using the letters of the acronym to construct a new word, *eatmu*. Simply saying *eatmu* either out loud or only in your mind can be an effective way to respond to these thoughts. Just say *eatmu*, pause for a moment to experience the impact of its meaning, and then turn your attention elsewhere. *Eatmu* will quickly convey the richness of our deep forgiveness language and understanding directly into the unforgiving part of your heart. Over time with more repeated messaging, the sought-after heart change will occur. *Eatmu* is our one-word answer to the riddle of the inner psychological Sphinx of unforgiveness.

In the next chapter, we will discover how our definition of forgiveness can be made even more effective by personalizing it for your brain.

4. YOUR PERSONAL BRAIN

Have you ever noticed that when things are said one way to some people they don't get it, but when explained in a different but equivalent way they do? Teachers experience this with students all the time. Spouses often find it in their communication with each other. This is because your language, by which you comprehend the world, is deeply personal. Everyone, even speakers of the same cultural language, uses a different set of words and meanings, depending on their individual learning experiences. The words you know and the ways they can be arranged into sentences personally meaningful to you are uniquely stored in your brain.

Moreover, everything you have ever learned is contained in your brain, the huge network of interconnected neurons inside your head, which speak to each other by sending electrochemical signals back and forth. The way you perceive, understand, and experience the world is determined by this flow of information. Whenever you learn something new, or come to think, feel, or see things differently, it is because your brain has changed its neural connections within, altering the signals transmitted between neurons.

Forgiveness is then personal brain change. When your thoughts become more forgiving and your feelings less angry, it is because the language you have used to forgive has reached primarily that part of your brain which is your emotional center, figuratively referred to as your heart, and secondarily that part which is your philosophical mind. When this happens, the neurons which store unforgiveness are altered so that the unforgiveness is released.

The language of deep forgiveness, which we have been developing, may be made even more effective by personalizing it for each person. For example, let's do this with the Basic View of our definition of forgiveness, beginning with the first pillar:

A. "You don't have to *make up for what you did to me.*"

Let's substitute the italicized part of the statement with alternative phrases which are either close in meaning or provide more specifics. Several examples are listed below. The first two are very similar to the original. The last five are particular ways in which a partial restitution might be made. Think of someone you need to forgive as you read each one.

"You don't have to *give me back what you took from me.*"
"You don't have to *pay me back for what you cost me.*"
"You don't have to *take responsibility for the harm you caused me.*"

4. Your Personal Brain

"You don't have to *acknowledge how you wronged me.*"

"You don't have to *confess your sins against me.*"

"You don't have to *repent and be fair to me.*"

"You don't have to *apologize for what you did to me.*"

Jennifer thought that she had given up any hope for restitution, thinking that it just wasn't possible anyway. *There was no way he could ever make it up to me.* But in reading the list above, she became aware that a part of her was still waiting for him to acknowledge how badly he had wronged her. Hanging on to this small, yet significant means by which he could make partial restitution was a hidden block to greater forgiveness freedom. Once it was uncovered, she was able to practice letting go of it using her personal variation of Statement A.

As you read through the list above, did you notice any part of yourself still insisting on some kind of partial restitution, like Jennifer? Did any of the variations provoke an emotional response from you such as, *But I DO still demand that!*? Did any of them feel more impactful than the original statement? The last five statements, by letting go of your demand for the offender to admit moral wrongness, may cause you to experience the Acceptance Conundrum profoundly. See if you can make up your own variation that fits your specific situation better.

Now, let's do the same thing for Statement B:

B. "I don't have to *hurt you for hurting me.*"

Below is a list of variations of this statement, with phrase substitutions in italics. Again, think of the person you need to forgive as you read each one.

"I don't have to *get even with you*."
"I don't have to *take my pound of flesh*."
"I don't have to *pay you back for what you did*."
"I don't have to *show you how it feels*."
"I don't have to *give you a taste of your own medicine*."
"I don't have to *make you regret ever crossing me*."

When Mike, another forgiveness seminar participant, read through this list, he had little reaction until he got to the last variation. This last one had sudden impact on him, compelling him to cry out, "But I DO want them to regret ever crossing me!" A wide grin spread across his face, revealing a bit of embarrassment regarding his spontaneous self-disclosure. I smiled back and replied, "Well, you may not have fully forgiven them then."

As you read through the list above, did you notice any difference in your emotional response to each variation? Were you surprised by how resistant you felt saying one of them, like Mike? Did any feel more impactful than the original statement? See if you can make up your own variation that fits your particular situation better.

The responses of Jennifer and Mike illustrate how small

changes in phrasing can have a potentially big effect on how well your heart can hear your intention to forgive. They show the power of putting things into different words. If you were able to identify or create personally powerful phrase substitutions, let's try them out using the Expanded View. Use them to fill in the blanks below:

Forgiveness is having an attitude toward the offender which both states:

A. "Although it would be the right thing to do, you don't have to _____."

B. "Although it would be a fair thing to do, I don't have to _____."

Now read your new personalized variations to see if you notice any deeper emotional impact. Relief and resolution mean you are using the right language to reinforce forgiveness in your heart. Resistance is especially good in showing you where you must dig to practice more productively.

Now try your personalized variations again using the Full View:

Forgiveness is having an attitude toward the offender which both states:

A. "I accept that you will never _____, although it would be the right thing to do."

B. "I accept that I will never _____,

although it would be a fair thing to do."

Did you notice any difference in your response to the two different views? What were the effects of the particular words used? How did they impact your heart in unique ways?

Many of us work out regularly to stay in shape. We go to the gym to practice our training routine, a set of exercises to tone and strengthen our muscles, such as aerobics and weight lifting. After working with a routine for a while, we often reach a plateau where progress becomes slow. Personal trainers tell us that at this point we must vary our routine to work out slightly different muscle groups to make further gains. Likewise, varying the language you use to practice forgiveness will affect slightly different groups of neurons that store unforgiveness, enabling you to continue making progress. Rotating the variations and phrase substitutions you use over time will deepen their effect.

Now that we have thoroughly explored the language of deep forgiveness and understood its essential meaning, you can wrap up the concepts you have learned by keeping them in mind as you say to yourself out loud several times, *This is what I mean when I say, "I forgive."* I call this a concept wrapper that strengthens the neurological connections between the sentence, "I forgive," and its underlying concepts. Saying it out loud allows the neurons in your auditory system to also participate in the reinforcement as you hear yourself speaking. The next time you say, "I forgive," it will be said with much more depth and conviction.

In the next chapter, we will examine what forgiveness does NOT mean.

5. WHAT FORGIVENESS IS NOT

Have you heard any of the following said or implied?

If you have really forgiven me, then …
> you'll excuse my behavior.
> you'll permit me to continue my behavior.
> you'll let me back into your life.
> you'll forget all about it and act like nothing has happened.
> you'll not feel hurt anymore over what I did.
> you'll like me and be nice to me.
> you'll not care whether I face any consequences for my behavior.

The statements above represent common misconceptions about forgiveness, due in part to unrealistic teaching from well-meaning but overly idealistic teachers. Unfortunately, these confusions can be used by some to manipulate others for their own interests.

Let's clarify our understanding of forgiveness by examining

what it does not mean. Specifically, forgiveness is not: *excusing bad behavior, condoning bad behavior, offering to reconcile, forgetting what happened, taking away the hurt, liking the offender,* or *sacrificing justice.* I will briefly comment on each one.

Forgiveness is not *excusing bad behavior.* We may be hesitant to forgive, worried that we might be implying that what the offender did is *really okay,* or *not that bad, considering.* This discomfort is caused by lumping together existential and moral acceptance, creating the Acceptance Conundrum. But we have learned how to resolve this dilemma by accepting or tolerating the offender's existence, while morally rejecting their choices, actions, and character. Forgiveness does not minimize the badness of the behavior.

Forgiveness is not *condoning bad behavior.* It does not give permission for the bad behavior to continue. It does not diminish our ability to establish our boundaries, to say no and decide what we will or will not permit into our lives. Forgiveness allows for the defense of self and others.

Forgiveness is not *offering to reconcile.* Reconciliation requires more than just forgiveness. Broken trust has to be rebuilt over time, if ever. We can choose to have no relationship with people we have forgiven, especially if they are abusive or dangerous.

Forgiveness is not *forgetting what happened.* Contrary to what some believe, it is impossible to intentionally forget a significant injury! (see Appendix). But even if we could, we wouldn't want to lose any valuable lessons learned from the experience, such as how to identify untrustworthy people. Also, it seems self-evident that we can only forgive what we remember. Forgiveness does not obligate us to act as if nothing happened.

Forgiveness is not *taking away the hurt*. Hurt can remain after forgiving the offender. It simply says that what was done to us was wrong and that we have been injured as a result. It is still valid. The pain needs to be healed, but that healing is a separate process. Forgiveness may help but doesn't necessarily take all the pain away. It doesn't automatically make everything *all good now*.

Forgiveness is not *liking the offender*. Even if we previously liked the offender, our later experience with them may have revealed personality traits which we dislike. Even after we have forgiven them for the offense, our dislike of who they have shown themselves to be may remain.

Forgiveness is not *sacrificing justice*. We may feel that the offender does not deserve to be forgiven and that justice is being sacrificed by our forgiveness. But remember we only have the authority to forgive at the personal level. The offender may still face consequences at the societal level, and certainly at the universal level. In forgiving, we set aside our pursuit of justice and leave it to the courts or to God. Justice will not be left undone at the end.

Forgiveness is naturally hard. But it is made even harder when its definition is extended far beyond the Two Pillars, creating unnecessary burdens for forgivers. Ironically, this can create resistance to forgive, by asking for more than the forgiver can accept. Frustrated would-be forgivers give up and say they just can't do it. It is important to be clear on what forgiveness is not.

In the next chapter, we will review and add detail to our Two Pillars metaphor.

6. THE TWO PILLARS

During the course of this book, we've explored many concepts to help us to forgive more deeply and quickly. Now it is time to summarize and organize them in a memorable and accessible manner, by developing a full description of the metaphor of *the Two Pillars*. Forgiveness is pictured as a crossbeam, held up by two pillars, representing its two core aspects or attitudes. Pillar A sets aside the Law of Restitution, while Pillar B sets aside the Law of Retribution. The Two Pillars stand upon the critical foundation that is the resolution to the Acceptance Conundrum, existential accepting the morally unacceptable, as illustrated in the next figure. Since a very large portion of our brain is used to process vision, approximately 50% according to brain researchers, seeing this diagram will engage many more of our brain neurons to learn the concepts fully and make them easier to recall and apply.

Figure 1: The Two Pillars

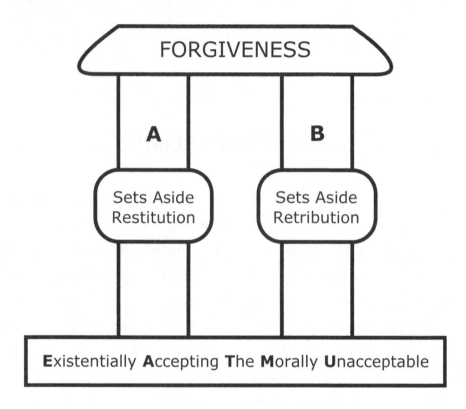

Imagine that you are a tourist visiting just such a pillared structure built during ancient times. Facing it from the north, you see a view similar to that shown in the figure and draw a sketch of it in your notebook. As you circle around the structure, you make more sketches from the west, south, and east. When you are done, your notebook contains a total of four distinct sketches made from four different views.

Similarly, our Four Views of the definition of forgiveness are distinctive perspectives on the same Two Pillars which represent our two core forgiving attitudes toward the offender, as summarized in the table below.

Table 1: The Four Views of the Two Pillars

View	The Two Pillars of Forgiveness
Legal	A. "I choose to set aside the Law of *Restitution* at the personal level and let go of my demand that it be enforced." B. "I choose to set aside the Law of *Retribution* at the personal level and let go of my demand that it be enforced."
Basic	A. "You don't have to make up for what you did to me." B. "I don't have to hurt you for hurting me."
Expanded	A. "Although it would be the right thing to do, you don't have to make up for what you did to me." B. "Although it would be a fair thing to do, I don't have to hurt you for hurting me."
Full	A. "I accept that you will never make up for what you did to me, although it would be the right thing to do." B. "I accept that I will never hurt you for hurting me, although it would be a fair thing to do."

Let's briefly review the differences between the Four Views. The Legal View communicates to the heart by way of the mind, using precise legal language so that you may understand exactly what you are doing by forgiving. The Basic View uses simple, concise, child-like words to speak directly to the heart in a manner that it can readily hear. The Expanded View builds upon the Basic View by adding moral clauses which relieve the tension caused by the Acceptance Conundrum, making it easier for the heart to accept its message. The Full View rewrites the Expanded View, adding words *accept* and *never* to give it an emotional impact with a sense of finality. Each of the Four Views affects the heart differently and has individual benefits in different people.

Now let's return to our tour of the two-pillar structure. As you walked around it, you saw the gradual changes in your view of the pillars between the four you drew. These countless other perspectives represent the many possible personal variations of our forgiveness language we explored. You may have also noticed some big boulders standing upright just behind the foundation, appearing like part of the structure, until you saw them more clearly from a different angle. These represent the things we may have once assumed were a part of forgiveness, but upon closer inspection realized are not.

Use this mental picture of the Two Pillars metaphor to hold together the interrelated concepts underlying forgiveness in your mind to aid you on your journey. Say to yourself again, *This is what I mean when I say, "I forgive."*

CONCLUSION

Jennifer had feared being forever stuck with her bitterness and resentment. Yet she was so relieved to be finally making progress in forgiving her abuser by working through the concepts in this book. She learned how to speak forgiveness in her mind using words which impacted her heart. She felt much less burdened in the understanding that letting go of her demand for restitution didn't mean she couldn't still wish for it. Most importantly, Jennifer discovered how to resolve the Acceptance Conundrum by existentially accepting the morally unacceptable, allowing her to move forward through a once seemingly insurmountable obstacle. She learned how to get relief from her obsessive unforgiving thoughts by gently disrupting them using the special word, *eatmu*. By experimenting with her forgiveness language, Jennifer uncovered some subtle areas of unforgiveness in her heart, enabling her to work specifically on them. Lastly, she found greater peace in realizing that forgiveness was not excusing bad behavior, invalidating her hurt, or sacrificing justice. Jennifer had made tremendous progress indeed.

But her forgiveness journey was not yet complete. Unforgiving thoughts still bothered her, although they appeared far less frequently. Her anger was a lot less intense than it used to be. She wished she could get her abuser completely out of her mind but didn't know what more to do. A large part of the problem was that he reminded her of her mother and this triggered old wounds, making it especially difficult for her to fully be free of her anger toward him. Jennifer continues to move forward, wishing her forgiveness journey could go faster, but she's also very grateful for how far she's come.

Forgiveness is often thought of as the letting go of anger, but I see the reduction of anger more as a sign that forgiveness has taken hold. It is the fruit of forgiveness rather than the forgiveness itself. The core of forgiveness is defined by its two essential aspects, which set aside the Laws of Restitution and Retribution. The letting go of anger, bitterness, and resentment depends upon the degree to which these core pillars can be said and meant. It is not possible to simply turn off our feelings by an act of will. Lasting desirable emotional change is the result of making the right adjustments in attitude and belief. Focusing too narrowly on not being angry may lead to frustration or repression instead of the true deep forgiveness we desire.

On the forgiveness journey, people can get impatient with themselves. They may feel guilty about their slow progress, thinking: *I should be over this by now; there must be something wrong with me*, or *Maybe I'm just not a good Christian*. The situation is only made worse by misapplying the oft-quoted admonition by Jesus:

> "For if you forgive other people when they sin against you, your heavenly Father will also forgive you. But if you do not forgive others their sins, your Father will not forgive your sins." (Matt. 6:14)

When Jesus spoke these words, he was proclaiming to the hearers of his day the establishment of a higher spiritual ethic; the good news of a new covenant centered on forgiveness had arrived. His followers were to set aside at the personal level the Natural Laws of Restitution and Retribution and embrace forgiveness as a way of life. Having a forgiving heart would be a sign of their relationship with him. Jesus' statement was aimed toward those who had not yet decided to keep his teaching, not at those already trying to forgive. It was meant to wake up the inattentive and complacent, not to burden the struggling forgiver. It was to be interpreted not as a strict exchange or *quid pro quo*, but as an invitation into fellowship with him.

No one knows the human condition better than Jesus. Once the father of a demon-possessed boy came to Jesus, asking *if* Jesus could help his son. Their subsequent exchange and Jesus' response afterward is revealing:

> " 'If you can'?" said Jesus. "Everything is possible for one who believes." Immediately the boy's father exclaimed,

"I do believe; help me overcome my unbelief!" (Mark 9:23-24)

Jesus saw the man's belief within his struggle to believe and counted it as acceptable. He honored his request and casted the demon out of the boy. When we come to Jesus with our struggle to forgive saying: *I do forgive; help me overcome my unforgiveness!*, he responds in a similar manner, deeming our forgiveness acceptable. Jesus knows how hard it is for us to forgive and empathizes with our difficulties. If you truly want your heart to adopt the attitudes of the Two Pillars, then your forgiveness is already honorable to him.

Now that you understand the context and intent of Jesus' admonition, don't let others misuse it to hit you over the head. And don't do it to yourself, either. You don't need the extra guilt and the headache! Instead, you can just tell yourself and others: *That admonition doesn't apply to me because I'm trying my best to forgive from my heart and Jesus knows that it is a process.*

Some people think of forgiveness in black and white terms, asking themselves: *Have I forgiven yet?* The better question to ask is: *How much have I forgiven?* Forgiveness is indeed a process, much like the weather. During the middle of winter, we expect the temperature to gradually rise until the middle of summer. But on any given day, the temperature may be higher or lower than the previous day's. Likewise, the practice of forgiveness creates a positive trend, but there will be significant fluctuations along the way. Do not let the days of feeling less forgiving

Conclusion

discourage you, because they are an expected part of the process. It takes time for all the necessary neurological changes to happen. Re-read this book regularly and practice the exercises to further absorb the material and quicken your pace.

Our exploration of the language of deep forgiveness has yielded many practical insights into how to forgive deeper and faster. But this is just the beginning. Beyond the Two Pillars and the Acceptance Conundrum, other topics related to forgiveness need to be understood to complete our forgiveness journey. Some of these include: controlling rage, dealing with obsessive thoughts and traumatic memories, PTSD, self-forgiveness, and spirituality. I will cover them all thoroughly as I release the next books in my ForgiveWell Series.

If you have found our journey together enlightening, would you do me the great favor of posting a **5-star rating** and/or review on Amazon to help new readers discover the benefits of this book? It will only take a minute and be such a blessing to them! I would *really* appreciate it. You can also help by leading a small group study using the Study Guide in the Appendix and sharing this material with your pastor and other church leaders.

Please visit ForgiveWell.com to sign up for my newsletter to stay in touch and be notified of new book releases and special video webinar events where we might talk live. There you will find a book sample webpage that you can share on social media. You can also contact me directly through the contact page. I would love to hear your story of how my material has been impacting your life, work, or ministry. It is so encouraging to hear and inspires my future research and writing. If you would like to participate in my creative process by sharing your story with me that would be a wonderful blessing. Those interested in my spiritual life coaching service can also contact me there.

It will take all of us working together to help more people find their way past the distractions of life to the deep knowledge that is good for the soul and our world. So much wasted mental energy and tragic violence can be avoided by forgiveness made easier.

ForgiveWell's mission is to transform the Church and the world, one forgiver at a time. **This lofty goal could be swiftly accomplished if everyone who reads this book tells just two other people about it!!!** Thank you so much for your help in spreading this knowledge of how to forgive deeply and quickly so that we can all live with inner peace, happiness, and spiritual vitality! Our motto indeed is "Forgive well to live well!"

APPENDIX

Dictionary Definitions of Forgiveness

Let's see what we can learn about forgiveness by consulting modern English and theological dictionaries. *Webster's Dictionary* definition of the word *forgive* is:

1. to give up resentment against or the desire to punish; stop being angry with; pardon
2. to give up all claim to punish or exact penalty for (an offense); overlook
3. to cancel or remit (a debt)

Webster's definition is helpful in telling us that the word *forgive* has several usages. The first usage is about the letting go of anger, the second retribution, and the third restitution. The last two correspond to our two core pillars of forgiveness, while the first is a measure of their outcome.

Definitions of forgiveness from three top theological dictionaries are listed below:

1. The act by which an offended party removes an offense from further consideration, thereby reestablishing a basis for harmonious relations with the offender. (*New Interpreter's Dictionary of the Bible*)[1]

2. The wiping out of an offense from memory; it can be affected only by the one affronted. Once eradicated, the

offense no longer conditions the relationship between the offender and the one affronted, and harmony is restored between the two. (*Anchor-Yale Bible Dictionary*)[2]

3. A dynamic, social-psychological experience of being released from the deleterious effects of guilt and sinful behavior and restoring broken relations between human beings and God and among themselves. (*Dictionary of Jesus and the Gospels*)[3]

These theological definitions seem overly abstract, impractical, and idealistic. The first one goes too far in extending the bounds of forgiveness. A forgiven offense can be given further consideration regarding how much to trust the offender going forward. You might forgive someone of stealing money from you, but you wouldn't then put him in charge of the church treasury! The second one expands the definition beyond reason. Memories can't be erased, and the offense can't be eradicated from history. Memories may indeed condition the future relationship. Trust has to be earned back, if even possible. Forgiveness is not automatic reconciliation. The third definition is the best of the three, but it is so abstract that it is not practically useful. No wonder there is so much confusion in the Church about forgiveness!

Study Guide

1. What elements of Jennifer's story did you identify with the most?

2. What is the Acceptance Conundrum, and how do you resolve it?

3. The following table lists the Four Views of the definition of forgiveness used in this book. For each view, read both pillar statements while keeping in mind someone you need to forgive. What was your experience of each statement? How did it differ between views?

View	The Two Pillars of Forgiveness
Legal	A. "I choose to set aside the Law of *Restitution* at the personal level and let go of my demand that it be enforced." B. "I choose to set aside the Law of *Retribution* at the personal level and let go of my demand that it be enforced."
Basic	A. "You don't have to make up for what you did to me." B. "I don't have to hurt you for hurting me."

Study Guide

Expanded	A. "Although it would be the right thing to do, you don't have to make up for what you did to me." B. "Although it would be a fair thing to do, I don't have to hurt you for hurting me."
Full	A. "I accept that you will never make up for what you did to me, although it would be the right thing to do." B. "I accept that I will never hurt you for hurting me, although it would be a fair thing to do."

4. Choose one of the views above. Can you change any of the words or phrases to make it more meaningful or emotionally impactful to you in your personal situation?

5. Is it okay to still wish for restitution after forgiving someone?

6. How does the distinction between laws and principles, as discussed in the chapter on the two Natural Laws, help you solve dilemmas regarding forgiveness?

7. Have you observed situations in which the meaning of forgiveness was extended too far beyond its core pillars into something unhealthy?

8. How have concepts in this book helped you to move

forward on your forgiveness journey? Did you experience any *ah-ha* moments?

REFERENCES

2. Two Natural Laws

[1] D. P. O'Mathúna, "BODILY INJURIES, MURDER, MANSLAUGHTER," *DOTP*, 93.
https://accordance.bible/link/read/IVP-Pentateuch#1463

[2] "ἀφίημι ἄφεσις παρίημι πάρεσις," *TDNT (Abridged)*, 88.
https://accordance.bible/link/read/TDNT#1117

Dictionary Definitions of Forgiveness

[1] STEPHEN WESTERHOLM, "FORGIVENESS," *NIDB*, paragraph 17486.
https://accordance.bible/link/read/New_Interpreter's_Dictionary_of_Bible#17486

[2] John S. Kselman, "FORGIVENESS.," *AYBD*, 2:831.
https://accordance.bible/link/read/Anchor#40027

[3] F. S. Spencer, "FORGIVENESS OF SINS," *DJG*, 284.
https://accordance.bible/link/read/Dict._of_Jesus_&_Gospels_(2nd_Ed.)#3787

ABOUT THE AUTHOR

Dr. Allen Gee has dedicated his life to helping others reach their spiritual best by embarking on a journey of deep forgiveness to inner peace, happiness, and enlightenment. He has a doctorate in clinical psychology from Trinity College of Graduate Studies and did his clinical training at Fuller Theological Seminary and Hope International University. Dr. Allen studied theology at Fuller and the art of spiritual guidance at Christian Formation and Discipleship Ministries. He also has an extensive scientific and engineering background in physics and artificial intelligence, having done research at Caltech, Jet Propulsion Laboratory, and in the defense aerospace and investment trading industries.

Dr. Allen can be reached online at ForgiveWell.com.

Made in the USA
Coppell, TX
23 July 2024

35112435R00049